Quality Customer Care

by

Joan Scott

GW00695657

ISBN 0 948680 26 1

The Author

Joan Scott has spent most of her working life in social work, initially in Residential Child Care for NCH and later in the management of Residential Provision for Barnardo's.

She has been both training officer and college lecturer and latterly as a freelance trainer been involved in training staff who work with the elderly. At present most of her training is directed toward Wardens of Sheltered Housing and Work-based Assessor training for NVQ.

Acknowledgements

Thanks to Jenny Inglis and her colleagues in Consumer Services, Solihull MBC.

Joan Scott   *September 1992*

Contents Guide

Dedication: To my Mother and Father

Part One

Customer First

Customer First is obviously about offering a quality service to our clients. They are the direct beneficiaries of the service we offer. However, because we so often work in conjunction with others or as part of a team, customer first is also about ensuring that we service our colleagues as best we can, so that they in turn can give a quality service to the clients. To that extent, our colleagues as well as our clients are our 'customers'.

We do not always think of our clients as customers and certainly hardly ever think of our colleagues as customers, but when we are looking at how to offer the best service possible to our clients, usually vulnerable people who rely on our best attentions, it is helpful to think in the language of 'customers'; it helps focus our minds on precisely what we are doing. In this booklet we shall explore what is meant by Customer First, what makes for quality service and how we can achieve and maintain 'satisfied customers'.

Quality

What do we mean by quality? We might say that it is a virtue or a value – it is 'good'-ness. But quality is something more concrete than that. It is a search for excellence and an attempt to provide services that fully meet the customers' requirements or needs.

Therefore offering a quality service is about finding how we can introduce the idea of virtue, value and 'good'-ness, even 'best'-ness into the service we offer to the customer, as well as making certain that the service is what the customer requires.

To develop a quality service, it is first of all vital to increase our knowledge about our customers and what they need. Unless an organisation 'knows' its customers and has clearly identified the customers' requirements, then it cannot provide a quality service. Methods for finding out what customers require are considered below.

Customers

You may be concerned by the use of the word 'customer' to describe those people to whom you offer a service. You may not like the term, preferring to think of them as residents or clients. This is natural. It is the way we have always referred to those people who expect to be the beneficiaries of the service we offer whether that service is in a residential setting, day centre or in the person's own home. However, I make no excuse for using the word 'customer', because I feel it not only describes a significant aspect of the relationship we have with the people we care for, but also makes us stop and think about exactly what we are doing.

In the future, when customers have more choice about where they will go for the services they require, those organisations that can offer the highest quality of service will have a strong advantage over the others in attracting customers. The care 'market', like any other, will have to give value for money and be constantly aware of the need for quality in the service it 'sells'.

Also, in addition to those people whom we might naturally think of as our customers, i.e. the clients, the residents, and even their families, there is another group of people whom I have already suggested are also our customers. This includes our colleagues, managers and other professionals. We can think of the first group as *external* customers and the second group as *internal* customers.

Standards

When we think of quality, we usually think of standards – high standards. Standards are something that we are all familiar with. The Kitemark of the British Standards Institute tells us that we can trust the goods to be of a certain standard. We may not know exactly what those standards are but we know they are there and the manufacturer must have achieved them for the product to receive the Kitemark. It gives us confidence in the product.

Many companies have based their reputation on manufacturing goods of a very high standard. Some brand names are synonymous with quality and high standards, for example Wedgwood, Marks and Spencer.

High standards are developed and maintained by having clear goals and by ensuring that all employees are working together towards the same goals. Therefore a successful organisation is the one with high standards of practice which gives a quality service to its customers.

There are two major factors which distinguish quality service from the merely adequate. The first is the personal aspect of service; it is about our behaviour and the way we personally react to others, in particular our customers. The second vital factor in providing a quality service is related to how the 'system' works (the 'process') and the worker's knowledge of it. Both these factors influence significantly the quality of service received by the customer; we shall discuss these in more detail later.

Where do we begin to improve the service we offer to our customers? The first stage is to consider our attitudes to our customers. Good customer service is as much about staff attitudes as about the goods offered. Do the exercise and see for yourself.

Exercise 1

Think about an example of good service you have personally received recently, not in the work setting but in your private life. For example, do you have a garage that gives you excellent service? Or maybe it is a local shopkeeper who has given you good service. We expect the greengrocer to sell us fresh produce, but why do we choose to go to one greengrocer or market stall rather than another?

When you have thought of an example, write down some of the things that make you say that this was good service.

Now think of an example of bad service that you have experienced recently. Again, it may have nothing to do with the quality of the goods purchased. It may be that you have been in a shop waiting to be served and the shop staff have kept you waiting for no apparent reason, while they were talking over last evening's television programmes.

Again, when you have thought of your example, identify those things in the situation that make you say this was poor service.

Comment

One of the most common things people say when asked to identify what it is that makes for good or bad service is that it is all about attitudes. This is true, but we need to be more precise than that. What do we mean by attitudes?

Some of the words associated with good service are:

> friendliness
> punctuality
> consideration
> being treated as an individual
> courtesy
> commitment
> honesty
> integrity
> keen to help and to please
> patience
> ability to listen
> showing interest

The list could go on, but what is emerging is a way of behaving that makes the customer feel that they are important as people and are not just a number or a hindrance to the flow of the day.

If we analyse what are the main features in bad service, the list of words we use may be the opposite of those above.

> unfriendliness
> uncaring
> impatience
> lateness
> not listening
> obviously disinterested
> being rude

Compare these lists with the lists you have made. To what extent do they coincide?

The right attitudes, then, are expressed as ways of behaving which say to those people we serve that the service we offer puts our customers first and that we are constantly trying to improve our service and give them a little more than they expect.

Expectations

Customer service, and whether it is judged to be good or bad, is based on the expectations of the customer. It does not matter how well we think we are doing in our attempts to give a good service, what really matters is how that service is viewed by the customer. The customer will usually have some expectations of the service that is being offered, i.e. what they think they *should* get. If the service exceeds the customer expectations, then the service will be judged to have been a good service. If however the service is less than the customer expected, then the service is judged to be a bad service. It is vital to identify exactly what the customer understands by a quality service in order that we can provide it. To give a quality service, it is essential that everyone has clear goals to aim for, and these must be linked to customer expectations. Most companies who strive to provide a high quality of service keep in close contact with their customers, using a variety of methods to obtain feedback about their service.

Go back to the exercise where you were thinking about services you have received and try to identify your own expectations in each of the situations you considered. There are some nationally well-known department stores which set very high standards of customer service and therefore we have very high expectations when we shop there. This leads us to another truth about Customer First, and that is that it is a constantly moving target. If each time I receive a service where my expectations are exceeded, then my expectations will increase.

So good customer service means always giving the customer a little more than they expect. The diagram overleaf highlights this more dramatically.

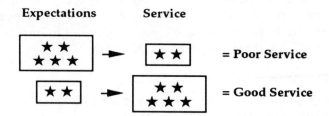

"Good customer service means giving our customers a little bit more than they expect"

Exercise II

In order to find out what your customers expect, you can undertake this research. Using the format below, write down what you think your customers expect from you. Then ask your customers what they expect from you. If you are providing good customer service, these two lists should be almost the same. However, there are often differences which may explain why, no matter how hard you try, you cannot please some of your customers.

What I think the customer expects of the service:

What the customer says they expect of the service:

Comment

You may think that your customer expects you to provide them with warmth, good food and activities to maintain their independence. However, they may really expect you to do everything for them and take all their cares and decisions away from them.

This can sometimes be seen when elderly persons move into residential care for the first time. They may well have been told by relatives and other professionals that, when they go into residential care, everything will be done for them. How upset they often are when confronted by a care assistant who asks them to do a bit of dusting or make themselves a piece of toast and a cup of tea!

Good customer service is a combination of two major factors. Firstly, there is the procedural aspect of customer care – the routines and systems and the way things happen – and, secondly, there is the personal aspect – how the individual service-giver gives the service. This latter is about behaviour, and we consider it first.

Behaviour

The way we behave towards the customer is a vital ingredient of the service we give to our customers and goes a long way to determining whether the service is 'good' or otherwise. We need therefore to think about our behaviour in a more detailed way; this next exercise helps you to analyse your behaviour.

Exercise III

On the next page is a questionnaire about behaviour. Read each pair of statements and tick the one that you consider to be most accurate for you. Think carefully about each of the statements – they are not all as simple and straightforward as you may at first think.

Of course it is impossible to say that there are right and wrong answers to this questionnaire because different ways of behaving might be appropriate in different situations. However, if we are trying to improve our customer service, then some answers seem to me to be far more appropriate than others.

11

Behaviour Questionnaire

1a How I behave influences how people behave towards me.	1b How I behave makes very little difference to the way people behave towards me.
2a I am as I am and people have to accept that.	2b I change the way I behave depending on who I am working with.
3a My feelings and behaviour just happen. I have no control over how I feel.	3b I can control my behaviour and my feelings.
4a I believe that people behave the way they do because their behaviour is inherited from their family.	4b I believe that people behave in the way they do because they have learned to behave in that way.
5a I have a choice in the way I behave towards people.	5b I have no choice in the way I behave towards people. It depends how I feel when I get up in the morning.
6a People's behaviour to me is largely governed by my behaviour towards them.	6b How I behave towards other people has no influence on how they will behave towards me.
7a I should think about the way I behave.	7b It is best to think about the task and to let behaviour happen naturally.
8a If people I work with upset me, I think about what their motives might be.	8b If the people I work with upset me, I try to think what circumstances may have brought this about.
9a I think it is best to speak your mind even if it hurts other people's feelings.	9b I think it is best to work at relationships and to use tact and sensitivity.
10a A well thought out plan can help me in my relationships with others.	10b I don't see the need to plan ahead. This stops the spontaneous reaction to situations.

Go through your responses to the questionnaire and compare your answers with my list – which seems to me to be the most appropriate in the context of customer care.

1a, 2b, 3b, 4b, 5a, 6a, 7a, 8b, 9b, 10a

Give yourself a point for each of your answers that agree with mine.

Comment

A score of *8-10* means that you are already very conscious of the power of your own behaviour.

5-8 means you are already beginning to think about ways of using behaviour to influence the way other people behave towards you.

A score of *less than 5* means that you may have to give some careful thought to learning more about behaviour and the effect it can have in our everyday dealings with other people.

A low score can mean a certain rigidity which you may have to work on. As workers with people, we need to be as flexible in our behaviour as is consistent with a planned approach.

Helping and Hindering Behaviour

Non-Verbal Behaviour and Body Language

First and foremost, we need to be aware of our own body language. This is the part of us that other people see and is often the first thing people notice about us. Long before people get to know what we think about things, what we like, what we do not like, etc., we will be sending messages to those about us through our body language. If we have a blank expression on our face when we are working with others, this may be seen as evidence of lack of interest, boredom, or a wish to be somewhere else!

Try turning the television sound down and just watch the picture; you can often make intelligent guesses about the content of the programme without hearing the voices because of the way actors are using their bodies.

"Albert Mehrabian found that the total impact of a message is about 7% verbal (words only) and 38% vocal (including tone of voice, inflection and other sounds) and 55% non-verbal."

"......the verbal component of a face-to-face conversation is less than 35% and that over 65% of communication is done non-verbally." (Alan Pease 1981)

If you can imagine working with a person who hardly ever looks at you directly but looks over your right shoulder at some point in the distance, who perhaps leans away from you and, if sitting, has their arms tightly crossed around their body, you might begin to get the feeling that this person is really not interested in you as a person. If you are talking to a person, telling them something that is important to you, and they look bored or keep glancing at their watch or start yawning, you again may feel that their interest in you is minimal, if it exists at all.

If we think about our non-verbal behaviour, it is possible to identify helping and hindering behaviours.

Exercise IV

Below, list all those non-verbal behaviours which you think might help to make your customers feel that you are interested in them and in giving them a good service.

Helpful non-verbal behaviours:

Verbal Behaviour – *What We Say*

In the same way that our non-verbal behaviour can help or hinder in our dealings with others, it is also possible to hinder or help with verbal behaviour, i.e. with what we actually say.

Exercise V

Think about the first exercise you did in this booklet. What were some of the verbal and non-verbal behaviours that helped make you say "this was a good service" and what verbal or non-verbal behaviours made you say "this was a bad service".

Helpful behaviour	*Hindering behaviour*
(a) *verbal*	(a) *verbal*
(b) *non-verbal*	(b) *non-verbal*

Comment

Some of the things you might have highlighted as helping behaviour could be:-

- smiling
- using names when you know them
- asking open questions
- verbal and non-verbal behaviour is congruent
- saying things that link to what the other person has said
- checking for understanding
- being genuine
- using touch if appropriate
- admitting not knowing something

Some of the things you might have highlighted as hindering behaviour could be:

- tone of voice
- not using your name although the other person knew it
- not asking questions that could have helped
- verbal and non-verbal behaviour being out of step
- sticking rigidly to saying things that are routine and standard
- not checking for understanding
- not looking at you
- being defensive

Listening

One of the greatest compliments we can pay another person is to listen carefully to what they have to say. Listening is a powerful way of telling someone that they matter and that their opinions count.

Listening is a skill which we need to learn. Although most people will say that they are 'good listeners', it is not always true. To be a good listener, we need to do more than just appear to be listening – we have to *look* and *sound* as if we are listening. This is how people know we are listening to them – this is *active* listening. Active listening is about hearing and understanding what is being said to us, summarising what we hear and reflecting back to the other person what we understand them to be saying. So, when I am listening actively, I may be nodding my head, looking directly with attentive eyes at who is talking, perhaps murmuring an occasional "yes", "I see" or "hmm", and possibly asking a relevant question or summarising what I have just heard.

This is not always easy. One of the commonest things about one-to-one conversations is that, whilst the other person is talking, we know that it is our turn to speak next; therefore we may not be listening carefully to what is being said because we are working out in our head what we will say when it becomes our turn. In practising customer care, we need to demonstrate that we are listening and that what our customer is saying is the most important thing that is happening to us at that time. And we can all do this using the appropriate verbal and non-verbal behaviour.

There are the 'go on' signals that we use: smiles, nods and other cues. It is also important to ask questions that encourage the other person to explore their thoughts and situations.

Most of us need to practise our listening skills and you might try with a colleague to experience what it feels like when you are not being listened to. You will find how quickly it is possible to feel angry and frustrated when your colleague does not give you the verbal and non-verbal cues that tell you that you are being listened to. This highlights why people may sometimes become aggressive and angry with us because they feel we are not listening.

Procedure

Procedure, in terms of customer care, is really about how things get done – the routines and systems that govern how the service is delivered. How are customers' needs met?

William B Martin, in his book *'Managing Quality Customer Service'*, lists seven areas of the procedural dimension of customer service.

1. *Timing* – Are you giving the service when people want it?

2. *Flow* – Is your service co-ordinated appropriately? How do you control the flow of the service to your customers?

3. *Flexibility* – Can your service be adapted to meet the various and perhaps changing needs of your customers?

4. *Anticipation* – Can you anticipate your customers' needs so that you can be one step ahead all the time?

5. *Communication* – How do you ensure that there is always good communication between staff and customers and between staff and staff?

6. *Customer Feedback* – How do you find out what your customers are thinking, in particular about what they want and what they think of the service you are giving?

7. *Organisation and supervision* – Is your service well organised and effectively supervised?

Timing and Flow

Firstly, how are the services delivered? What methods do you have for ensuring that all the different parts of the operation work together to provide a service that meets customer needs? This can be a very complex operation, with careful consideration being given to such things as rotas and the staff duty roster. The provision of good customer service can be hampered by conflicting timescales; for example, many customers who use day centre facilities may well enjoy their day and receive good service from the staff, but they may also find it very frustrating that they have to be ready to leave home very early in the morning to fit in with the transport timetable. Of course, there may be very little that can be done to ease this situation but, if the organisation is really wanting to provide a quality service, then feedback from the customer should be heeded and some form of action taken.

Flexibility

The service given to customers, particularly those customers who are vulnerable, should have the ability to meet their needs as nearly as it is possible to do. This raises the question of systems and who they are designed for. Think again about the example of transport to and from the day centre and consider who this system was designed for. Feedback from customers would indicate that they would like to be picked up later in the morning and not kept waiting in the late afternoon to be taken home. Can the process be varied? Is there some solution lurking somewhere that nobody has seen, that no one has ever thought about, perhaps because "we've always done it this way"? At the very least there could be an airing of the problem – perhaps listening to what the customers have to say will lead to a solution or at least a more tolerable acceptance of what cannot be changed.

Anticipation

Giving the customer more than they expected links to Martin's idea of anticipation. Can we plan ahead so as to anticipate the wishes of our customers? Workers in residential homes or in day care get to know their customers very well. They are, as it were, regulars! We also have a considerable amount of knowledge about how our customers might be expected to behave. Whilst this is vital, it can also be a disadvantage because the worker may feel that they can 'second think' their customers, based for example on a stereotyped image of an elderly person or of a mentally ill person. This may mean that it is not the individual needs of customers that are met, but rather the needs that the worker assumes to be those of the average elderly person or mentally ill person. Beware: there is no such thing as the *average* elderly person or *average* mentally ill person any more than there is an *average* teenager or an *average* married person or an *average* care assistant.

Communication

I have already commented very fully on personal communication between the customer and the worker and will comment later on the communication within organisations.

Customer Feedback

This is a vital part of the care worker's role and involves many of the basic caring skills, in particular the skill of listening, as previously discussed. It may appear simplistic to say that you should sit down with your customers and ask them what they think of the service you provide and how they think it could be improved. Simple it may be, but it is the beginning of customer feedback. Later we shall consider some slightly more sophisticated methods, but often the simplest can be the best. Collecting customer feedback should be seen as an important part of the caring job and what you find needs to be recorded somewhere and acted upon, otherwise it can be seen as an empty gesture and therefore dishonest.

Organisation and Supervision

These are fundamental to the provision of good customer service. If the organisation within the unit is haphazard, then no one will be clear about what happens when or who does what; the service to the customer will be far below that which the customer has the right to expect. It is vital to know what the procedures are. For example, in the case of a fire alarm, does everyone know what to do? Do you know where to go and how to ensure customer safety? In the case of suspected abuse, would you know how to proceed? These are fairly dramatic examples, but they demonstrate the importance of organisation, whether it is dealing with emergencies or making sure that the food is ordered in time for the cook to prepare the dinner at the time expected by the customer.

Managers have the overall responsibility for seeing that all parts of the organisation work together for the benefit of the customer. However, all workers need to know how the system works and how their part of the operation fits into the whole.

To provide quality customer service, both aspects, the personal and the procedural, have to be present. These two aspects are, or should be, closely intertwined.

Exercise VI

Think about the following situation and analyse it in terms of the seven factors listed above.

An elderly lady, accompanied by her daughter, arrives at a nursing home expecting to be received into the home for a brief period of recuperation. However, there is no one on duty who knows anything about it. Just as the Deputy is about to tell the daughter that there has been a mistake and the lady was not expected at the home on that day, a passing care assistant says that she thinks the arrangement was made when the Deputy was not on duty – but she is not sure!

The elderly lady is becoming more and more agitated and the daughter more and more irate. She says that she made the arrangement with the Home Manager the week before and had confirmed the booking by letter. The deputy is in a quandary. A request form should have been filled in with the elderly lady's details, but this seemed not to have been done . She could find no record. New residents' details were entered into the home's computer, but she did not know how to operate it and the clerk who did know was not on duty. None of the staff on duty apart from the one care assistant knew anything about the new admission.

The Deputy is becoming more and more angry herself with the daughter, who is demanding some action. The Deputy explains that, as there is no record of the elderly lady's admission, she has already given the only spare bed to someone else desperate for the service the nursing home could offer.

Altogether this is a very unhappy situation and not one that happens very often, but it helps to illustrate the importance in good customer service of well-planned procedures.

Comment

The first thing to note is the lack of anticipation and organisation. No one has made any attempt to manage the elderly lady's arrival at the home. There was a breakdown in communication in a major way. There was certainly plenty of customer feedback but, because of the confusion and anger, this was not constructive nor was it being listened to.

It is vital that workers behaves in a sensitive way in working with customers. However, if the workers are unaware of the procedures or if the procedures are unclear, then customers are going to become frustrated and angry; they will feel very strongly that they are not receiving the service they deserve or have the right to demand. Such an experience could influence significantly the attitude of the customer towards the organisation and staff. If they had a choice, they could well exercise it by going elsewhere. At the very least, it will influence the degree of care the customer feels they can expect in the future.

Part Two

The Internal Customer

So far we have been considering the 'external customer' who is the easily identified beneficiary of our service, namely the resident or client and perhaps also a relative. Now we turn to another group of people who, as suggested earlier, are as much our customers as client or relative. Of course it may be difficult initially to think of our colleagues as customers and it will probably be even harder to think of our managers as customers. However, if we are to provide a service that puts the customer first, we must also consider our internal customers, both colleagues and management. If you think of colleagues and managers as people for whom you provide a service as well as your external customers, then you will begin to see the advantages for customer care in thinking in this way.

Exercise VII

Pause now and list those people whom you consider to be your 'internal customers':

Comment

You will no doubt have listed colleagues, people you work most closely with, but there are others. Immediate line managers are also your customers! It is true that no one can do all the tasks it takes to run a complex organisation, whether it is the massive ICI or a small nursing home for elderly persons or a lunch club relying on volunteer effort. Each worker relies on others doing their job well. If one person fails to do the right thing at the right time, there can be terrible consequences for other staff, and in the end the folk who will really suffer are the residents or clients. Care assistants depend on the manager to manage the unit so that they can do their job of caring for the day-to-day needs of the residents. The manager depends on the care assistants to do the caring and on the cook to do the catering, whilst they carry out their role of managing. This inter-dependency exists throughout the whole organisation, with each member of staff relying on other staff in order that the customer is cared for properly.

To illustrate this point, re-read the scenario in the previous section concerning the admission of a resident that no one seemed to know anything about.

Exercise VIII

Think through this scenario and identify some of the factors which, like the exercise you did when considering good and bad service at the beginning, contribute to poor internal customer service.

Comment

There are three major areas where the service we offer to colleagues and others within an organisation can run into difficulties; these are:

1. Communication
2. Systems and Procedures
3. Personal Support

Communication

It is vital to discuss within the staff team ways in which different parts of the organisation communicate with one another. Are there clear lines of communication? Do you know what those lines are?

In some organisations there are very strict lines of communication. For example, you may only pass information or receive information from your immediate line manager. Perhaps you cannot go straight to the boss with an interesting idea. Depending on the skill and sensitivity of the line manager, this can cause blockages in internal communications or, at the very least, stifle the emergence of new ideas and new ways of doing things.

When working together as a team, as opposed to just being a group of staff (and there is a difference!), it is important that there is a forum for staff to give each other feedback on the service they are providing, particularly to their internal customers – to each other. Just as it is important to create opportunities for customer feedback from the clients, it is also vitally important that there are opportunities for getting the staff team together to consider ways in which they could be better at what they do. Remember, customer care is a moving target and the team should be constantly working to improve the service and prepared to change what they do if that is necessary to meet needs that are changing.

Exercise IX

Consider at this point the communication system within your organisation.

List the opportunities you have for giving and receiving feedback from colleagues:

List some of the blocks to communication:

Comment

One of the most frequently quoted blocks to communication is the shift system, which means that many members of staff rarely work together or only meet briefly at the handover period, and that may be limited. This difficulty can be overcome partially by good record keeping, diaries, memos, duty books and staff meetings. At staff meetings it is useful to have a running agenda item that gives the staff team an opportunity to explore new ideas about how they can produce a better service for the customer.

A further block which makes communication difficult is what could be called 'professional jargon'. While jargon, or 'technical language' can be very necessary as an aid to accurate and efficient communication within any professional group, when viewed by someone who is not part of the profession it can serve to mystify and make things less clear and even incomprehensible. Social and health care is no different from any other profession and it has its own 'language'. Far better with clients and relatives to use simple and clear language; providing it is not patronising or 'talking down to them', this is always better because it aids communication and avoids making those who are not familiar with the jargon feel inferior or left out.

It is obviously impossible to give precise answers to what blocks might exist in your organisation, for every organisation is unique. However, ask yourself whether there are clear, simple lines of communication in your organisation. Has the most junior member of staff access to all the information they need and are there opportunities for them to share their knowledge with everyone else who ought to know? These are the sorts of questions we need to ask if the team or organisation is going to develop a thorough customer care philosophy.

Systems and Procedures

Every organisation, whether it is very large or quite small, needs systems and procedures – ways of doing things that ensure the organisation does what it is supposed to. Procedures are also important for ensuring that workers understand what their roles are and what the limits of their roles are. In many organisations procedures are dictated by legislation. For example, there are very clear procedures in Departments of Social Services for dealing with cases of suspected child abuse. This means that everyone knows what to do, who to contact and how to handle the situation.

In all organisations there are systems. Mostly they are in place to benefit the customer, but not always. Systems are interesting phenomena. They may be carefully thought out to ensure that customers receive the best possible service and lose none of their rights. However, there are systems which, like Topsy, just seem to have grown from nowhere. What often happens is that staff begin to behave in a certain way because it is easier, takes less time or is less stressful. This behaviour can become fixed and eventually develops into a 'system'. It can often be quite difficult after a while to say why the system has come to exist! "It seemed a good idea at the time!". Unfortunately, many of these unplanned systems often serve the worker more than the customer. How do *you* feel when you cannot get the service you want and you are told "It is standard practice!", especially when you can see that this is a plainly absurd way for an organisation to behave?

A typical example of this is trying to get a television repair person to visit at a time when you are at home to let them in. After being told several times that the company cannot tell the customer exactly when the engineer will call because he is so busy, or because he works from home, etc., etc., the sensible person begins asking why is it impossible to make arrangements in advance and agree a time? What is the difficulty in that? Many other people work on an appointment system and it generally works well. After being told again at length, the customer is not surprisingly very annoyed!

There are many other examples of 'systems' like this. Think of some of these informal and formal systems that operate in your organisation. One home for elderly persons had a system which insisted that residents went from the lounge to another part of the house at a set time each evening for a hot drink before bed. However, this took place long before most people would choose to go to bed. The only reason was that it prevented residents spilling tea on the lounge carpet. This is poor customer care. Do you have similar examples in your working situation?

Exercise X

Ask yourself:

How important are systems and procedures in your work setting?

How many systems exist through habit – it is the way it has always been done?

Think of one particular system and answer these questions:

- What is the purpose of the system?

- Is it designed with the customer in mind?

- How can it be improved?

- What flexibility, if any, do staff have when putting the system into practice?

Comment

With all systems and procedures it is vital to ask: "Who is benefiting from this system or this procedure?"; "Whose needs are being met through this way of working?" If it is the customer's, this is as it should be; if however it is the staff who benefit at the cost of the customer, then something needs rethinking.

What recommendations for change could you suggest?

Personal Support

This is vital if the organisation is going to have a good system of customer care throughout the organisation. It is very difficult for one individual to try to provide customer care if they are not receiving support from colleagues and the management. Customer care takes time as well as effort. It may mean you have to give that little bit longer to your customer and it is important that others understand this. Workers trying to give customer care need good supervision from their managers because this helps the worker to communicate their needs to their manager. Remember, you are the internal customer of the manager and asking for supervision to do your job more effectively is part of the service you require as a customer. In return, because the manager is also *your* customer, he or she will require a better and more thoughtful service from you on behalf of your customers.

Part Three

Customer Feedback Systems

Many commercial organisations now have systems which are designed to elicit feedback from their customers. The one we might be familiar with is the questionnaire that package holiday firms ask us to complete at the end of our holiday. This asks customers to say what they think about the service they have received. Of course, the effectiveness of this approach depends on the goodwill of customers in filling in the forms. If the holiday has been well organised and has met the expectations of the customers, they may be more likely to fill in the form. If the opposite is the case, the form may find its way into the rubbish bin!

Large organisations such as the Gas Board are asking their customers to complete simple questionnaires about the service they receive from their service engineers. The Abbey National Building Society prominently displays large posters in their branches advertising that they are seeking to provide a quality service to their customers. The Post Office carries out surveys to ascertain how promptly post is received by sending out a communication and asking the receiver to send it back with information about when it was delivered and at which postal delivery. Local authorities are also encouraging Community Charge payers to complain if things are not right, with slogans such as "If it's wrong, write it".

All these initiatives are being taken by organisations to ascertain customer expectations and to evaluate against those expectations the service that they offer. Earlier we considered customer expectations and noted that, if the service provided exceeds the customer's expectation, then that service is invariably considered good. Alternatively, a service that fails to exceed customer expectation is usually judged to be a poor serviuce. An example of service not exceeding expectations would be if, as a holidaymaker, we decided on a 4-star hotel because we wanted and therefore expected a little extra luxury, but found on arrival that the only reason the hotel had 4 stars was simply because each room had a mini-bar and colour television. If our expectation of luxury was greater than that, then we would designate that as poor service. On the other hand, perhaps you have experienced the holiday situation where the setting suggested a very basic service, but both the food and the way you were looked after turned out to be of the highest quality. These are the memorable occasions that we cannot wait to tell our friends about.

Many residential establishments and day care centres have committees of residents who, as well as organising activities within establishments, also act as representatives of the residents in feeding back to the staff what the residents think and feel about the service provided. However, one of the most effective ways of finding out what customers expect and what they feel about the service they are given is to ask them and to listen to their response. The care worker has an advantage because, generally, their customers are well known to them. This simple approach is usually far more effective in the care situation because many people do not have the inclination to fill in forms or questionnaires, particularly if they are long and confusing.

It is perhaps obvious that we should find out what the 'external' customer thinks of the service offered, but it is equally important to discuss with your 'internal' customers – your colleagues and managers – how they view the service they receive from you. How do you feedback to them your feelings about the service you receive from them as their 'internal' customer? Does a system exist for this to happen?

Exercise XI

How is customer feedback encouraged in your establishment? What are the procedures for customers to make complaints?

Comment

More and more organisations, whether they are residential homes, day centres, sheltered housing schemes, home care services, etc., are producing 'service-users' handbooks. These offer the service-user a range of helpful information, from the services offered by the organisation to what is available more widely in the local community. They also include detailed descriptions of the 'complaints procedure'. A customer needs to know at the outset how to make a complaint if the service is not what they anticipated. They need to know that their complaint will be

> a) listened to,
>
> b) handled with discretion, and
>
> c) acted upon.

No one is going to complain about a service if they think the complaint will be ignored or they will be victimised because of it.

Part Four

Reviewing Progress

In any kind of endeavour, it is essential to make provision for reviewing progress. This is a vital part of improving customer service. There has to be a procedure for the workers to feedback on their experience of providing a quality service to the customer. At the beginning of this book, the point was made that good customer service is a constantly moving target. Workers need time to take stock and to evaluate their practice in terms of the goals set for the service being offered. Is this what the customer requires, or have the customer's needs and expectations changed? What as a team do we need to do to improve the quality of our service?

This demands constant checking with customers, both external and internal, and it is obviously better if there is a procedure to ensure that it happens. Some groups have quality issues as a permanent item on the agenda of their staff meetings; other organisations have quality groups and quality circles. How it is done is less important than making certain it is done.

To complete this part of the booklet, there is one final task to be done. I suggest you draw up a Personal Action Plan. Think about the service you offer to your customers, both internal and external, and identify areas of that service that you could improve, even if only slightly. We are not trying to move mountains, only to change a number of things by small amounts that will improve the service. It is better – and easier – to change 1,000 things by 1% each than to try to change one thing by 1000%. Using the form shown overleaf, begin working on what you feel you can change, either something in your own behaviour or maybe part of the system that you have some influence or control over.

Write down what action YOU are going to take and set a date by which you will review your actions. This form could be kept by yourself or given to your supervisor and used in supervision.

The important thing to remember about customer care – and it is worth repeating it yet again – is that it is a constantly moving target and we cannot afford to be complacent, thinking we have got it right for all time. And remember, as our service to the customers improves, so their expectations will rise, and next time we have to try even harder.

References

Pease, Allan (1981) "Body Language", Sheldon Press

Martin, William B. (1989) "Managing Quality Customer Service", Kogan Page

Customer Care

Personal Action Plan

Subjects	Action	Review Dates